NATIONAL GEOGRAPHIC **OUR WORLD**

Stone Soup

A Folktale from France

Retold by Mary Quinn

NATIONAL GEOGRAPHIC LEARNING | CENGAGE Learning

This soldier is hungry. He doesn't have any food or money. But he has an idea.

The soldier puts some water and a stone in his pot.

The people ask, "What are you doing?"

The soldier says, "I'm making stone soup!"

The soldier tastes the soup.

"The soup is good," he says.
"But it needs a carrot or two."

The soldier asks a young woman, "Do you have any carrots?"

The young woman gives him some carrots. He puts them in the pot.

The soldier tastes the soup.

"The soup is good," he says.
"But it needs some beans."

The soldier asks an old woman, "Do you have any beans?"

The old woman gives him some beans. He puts them in the pot.

The soldier tastes the soup.

"The soup is good," he says. "But it needs some corn and a tomato or two."

The soldier asks a farmer, "Do you have any corn or tomatoes?"

The farmer gives him some corn and tomatoes. The soldier puts them in the pot.

The soldier tastes the soup and says, "Mmmm. Now the soup is ready!"

"May we have some soup?" the people ask.

The soldier shares the stone soup with the people.

It is very good!

Facts About Food

Some foods grow under the ground. Carrots and potatoes grow under the ground.

carrots

potatoes

Some foods grow above the ground. Tomatoes and grapes grow above the ground.

tomatoes

grapes

Do you know any other foods that grow under or above the ground?

Fun with Food

Color each food.
Then match the word to the food.

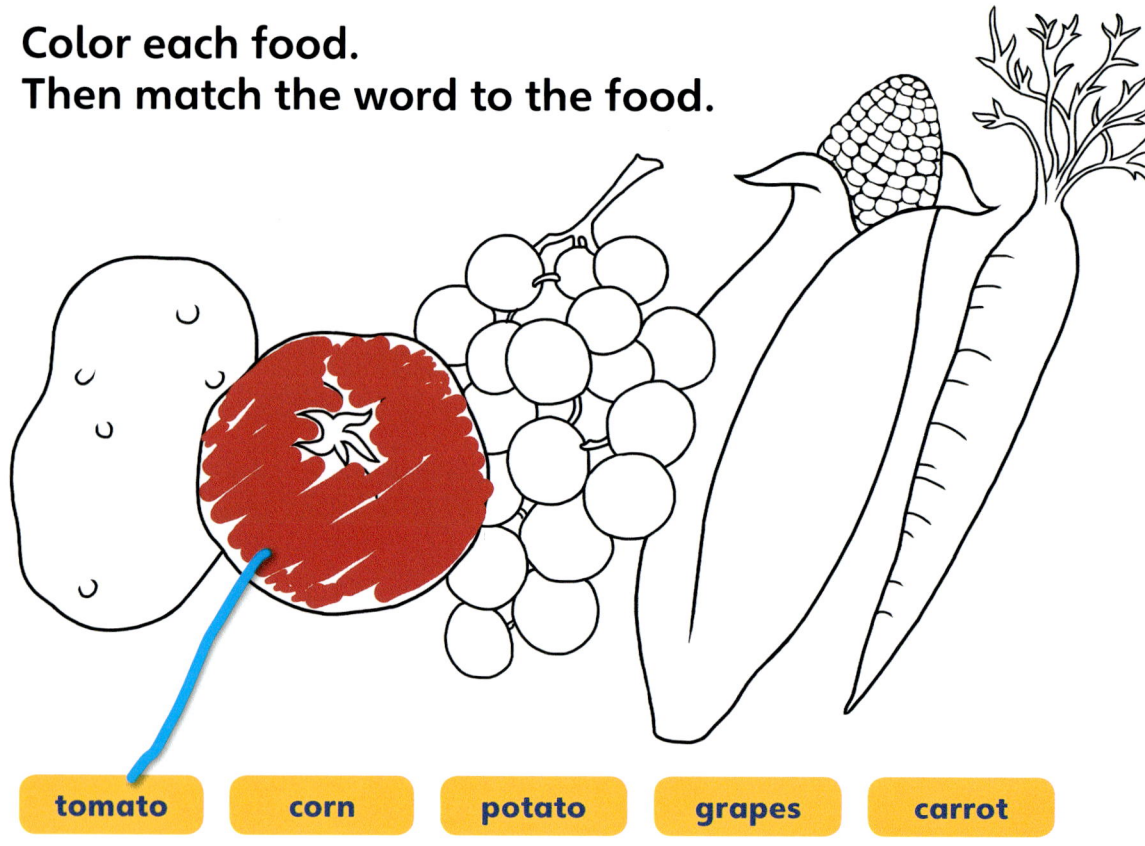

| tomato | corn | potato | grapes | carrot |

What foods do you see?
Write the name of each food.

carrot   beans   grapes
   potato   tomato

grapes

Glossary

idea

money

pot

shares

soldier

stone

tastes